Cornerstones of Freedom

Fort Sumter

Brendan January

CHILDREN'S PRESS®
A Division of Grolier Publishing
New York • London • Hong Kong • Sydney
Danbury, Connecticut

Library of Congress Cataloging-in-Publication Data

January, Brendan, 1972–
    Fort Sumter / by Brendan January.
      p. cm. — (Cornerstones of freedom)
    Includes index.
    ISBN: 0-516-20395-9 (lib.bdg.)   0-516-26227-0 (pbk.)
    1. Fort Sumter (Charleston, S.C.)—Siege, 1861—Juvenile
literature. 2. Charleston (S.C.)—History—Civil War, 1861–1865—
Juvenile literature. 3. Secession—South Carolina—Juvenile
literature. I. Title. II. Series.
E471.1.J36   1997
973.7'31—dc21
                                                        96-50143
                                                           CIP
                                                            AC

As dusk fell on December 20, 1860, the city of Charleston, South Carolina, burst into celebration. Excited crowds flooded the city streets. Church bells rang and firecrackers exploded.

The citizens of Charleston were celebrating because the state of South Carolina had seceded from, or left, the Union. The reasons for this separation were slavery and the right of Southern states to maintain their way of life. In the South, slavery had become an essential part of the Southern economy. Giant plantations relied on slave labor to harvest crops, such as cotton.

Citizens of South Carolina celebrate the news of the state's secession from the Union.

In the North, cities, factories, and railroads were being built at an amazing speed. The Northern economy was based on factory-produced goods. Millions of immigrants crowded into the Northern states in search of work and a better life. By the 1850s, many Northerners, called abolitionists, saw slavery as immoral and cruel. They pressured the federal government in Washington, D.C., to abolish slavery in every state. Southern slave-holders were furious. They believed that the government could not tell a state how to run its business.

One of the reasons for South Carolina's secession was the assertion that slavery was an important part of the Southern economy.

THE QUESTION

IF LINCOLN

will be elected or not, is one which interests all parties, North and South. Whether he

IS ELECTED

or not, the people of

SOUTH CAROLINA

(whose rights have been for a number of years trampled upon) have the advantage of supplying themselves with CLOTHING, at the well-known CAROLINA CLOTHING DEPOT, 261 King-street, at such prices as

WILL LEAD

them to be satisfied that the reputation of this Establishment has been

BOLDLY

and fearlessly maintained

FOR A

number of years, supplying its

SOUTHERN

Customers with all the Latest Styles, and at as low prices as any Clothing House in *the present*

CONFEDERACY

of all the States.

Thankful for the liberal patronage extended, the Proprietors desire merely to inform their customers and the public generally, that their present STOCK OF CLOTHING IS COMPLETE in all its departments, and are now prepared to offer Goods on the most reasonable and satisfactory terms. A call is therefore solicited by

OTTOLENGUIS, WILLIS & BARRETT,

November 5   261 King-street.

But then Abraham Lincoln won the presidential election in November 1860. Lincoln was a Northerner who promised to ban slavery from the western territories that were not yet states in the Union. South Carolina seceded after Lincoln's election and declared its independence from the United States. The secession celebration in Charleston continued for several days, but not everyone in the city joined the party.

Right: This poster in support of secession is really a clever advertisement for a clothing store.

Left: Abraham Lincoln

Major Robert Anderson was from the pro-slavery state of Kentucky, but he was fiercely loyal to the Union. He was considered to be the ideal person to command the troops in Charleston Harbor.

From a small fort called Fort Moultrie, Major Robert Anderson of the United States Army watched the blazing bonfires and celebrating crowds. News of the secession had already changed Charleston. The citizens took down

United States flags and regarded all federal soldiers with suspicion. Anderson began to feel like he was in a foreign country, and he worried that secession could lead to violence.

Anderson knew that Fort Moultrie's walls were too small and too weak to protect the soldiers against a secessionist attack. But on a small island in Charleston Harbor stood Fort Sumter. Completely surrounded by water, the large fort could provide much better protection for Anderson and his fellow soldiers than Fort Moultrie. Anderson considered moving his men to the fort.

Major Anderson knew that the walls of Fort Moultrie were not strong enough to withstand a Confederate attack.

Governor Francis Pickens

Although Fort Sumter was not yet ready for occupation by soldiers, Anderson knew that he and his men would be better protected by its high walls.

But Fort Sumter was still under construction. Although the strong brick walls towered 50 feet (15 meters) above the water, heaps of sand and stacks of wood littered the interior. Many of the fort's guns remained unmounted (not yet in position for defense). The fort stood empty except for some workmen and one guard.

Francis Pickens, the governor of South Carolina, was the leader of the newly independent "country." He studied Fort Sumter closely and realized how dangerous the fort could be if it was occupied by federal soldiers. If U.S. soldiers had access to the fort's powerful guns and cannons, they could easily close Charleston's harbor and crush South Carolina's

rebellion. Pickens ordered two guard ships to patrol the harbor. Armed with large cannons and eager volunteers, these ships had orders to destroy any ship that was seen carrying U.S. soldiers to Fort Sumter.

Major Anderson saw the guard ships and realized that moving his soldiers would be a big risk. If the guard ships spotted them, a war could break out between South Carolina and the United States. Uncertain about what to do, Anderson turned to Washington, D.C., for orders.

Charleston, South Carolina, was a quiet southern city before it became known as the city where the Civil War began.

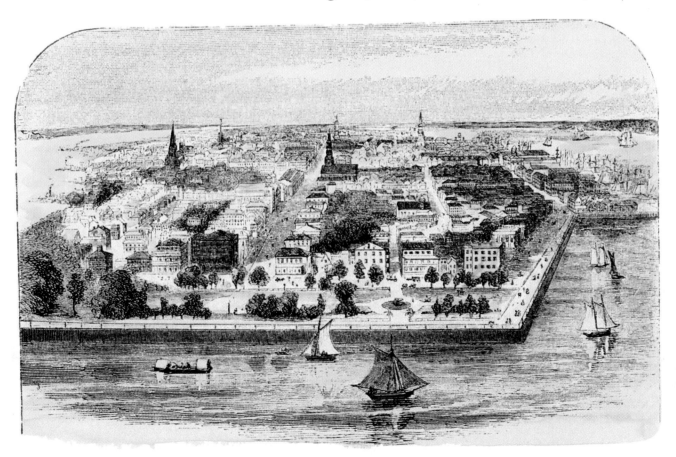

In Washington, President James Buchanan monitored the events in South Carolina with dismay. Lincoln had been elected president in November, but he would not move into the White House until the following April. For the next four months, James Buchanan was still in charge of the country.

President Buchanan knew that many Northerners were shocked by South Carolina's secession. The people demanded a strong response to the secessionists, whom they considered to be traitors to the United States government. But most of the people in the Southern states sympathized with South Carolina, and the leaders of many of those states also planned to secede from the Union. Buchanan's own advisers, many of them Southerners, advised him to be cautious in his response to the secessionists. Confused by many conflicting reports about the events occurring in South Carolina, Buchanan ordered Anderson to make his own decision whether or not to move the soldiers.

When Major Anderson received Buchanan's order, he decided to move his men to Fort Sumter. Anderson knew it was risky, but he feared that South Carolinians would take over the fort unless he moved quickly.

On the night of December 26, 1860, Anderson ordered the soldiers into two large rowboats. As

President James Buchanan

they rowed toward the fort, one of the guard ships spotted them. One of Anderson's officers ordered the soldiers to hide their guns beneath their coats and to keep rowing. Men on the guard ship used telescopes to watch the soldiers carefully. The Civil War could have started at that moment, but the officer's trick worked. The men on the guard ship did not see the soldiers' guns and, assuming that they were workmen, allowed the rowboats to pass. Minutes later, Anderson and his men landed at Fort Sumter and marched triumphantly inside.

Under the cover of night, Anderson and his men took over Fort Sumter in full view of Confederate guard ships.

The next morning, the people of Charleston saw the United States flag waving over Fort Sumter. Realizing that the fort was occupied, the people knew they had been tricked.

Two diplomats from South Carolina visited President Buchanan and demanded that he surrender Fort Sumter. Although Buchanan was surprised by Anderson's risky move, he did not agree to the diplomats' demand. They argued for many hours, but Buchanan would not give up Fort Sumter.

In the North, the occupation of Fort Sumter represented Union strength. Many Northerners were thrilled by Anderson's strategy. A writer in the *New York Tribune* noted that Anderson

Major Anderson (kneeling, with rope) raised the United States flag over Fort Sumter to signal its occupation by federal soldiers.

possessed "the highest order of military genius." Letters of support poured into Washington, D.C., from all over the North. In a letter to Anderson, Edmund Morris wrote, "The Lord bless your noble soul." Another man wrote, "while you hold Fort Sumter, I shall not despair of our noble, our glorious Union."

But tension grew in Charleston. The secessionists bitterly denounced Major Anderson. They started positioning guns and cannons that pointed toward Fort Sumter. Governor Pickens, shocked by Anderson's tactics, ordered that no mail or supplies be allowed to reach the fort. Anderson and his men were completely cut off.

President Buchanan knew that Anderson needed more food, supplies, ammunition, and soldiers, but he feared that if a ship was seen trying to reach Fort Sumter, it could cause a war. Buchanan decided to send a merchant ship, the *Star of the West*, to the fort. A merchant ship is used to transport goods and is not armed with guns or cannons. On January 5, 1861, the ship—loaded with soldiers and supplies—left New York City. Buchanan hoped that the secessionists in South Carolina would not fire on an unarmed ship.

President Buchanan ordered the Star of the West *to Charleston Harbor with food, supplies, and ammunition for the soldiers at Fort Sumter.*

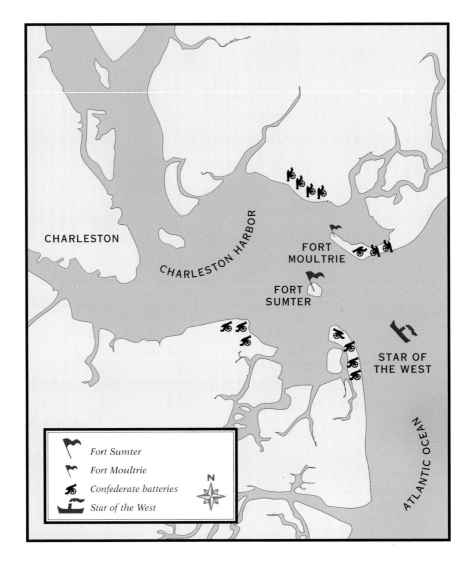

Fort Sumter was located in the middle of Charleston Harbor.

Four days later, the *Star of the West* arrived at the harbor in Charleston and approached the fort. Secessionist guard ships shot warning rockets into the air. Across the harbor, secessionist soldiers scrambled to their gun batteries. They loaded their guns and awaited the order to fire.

Inside Fort Sumter, an officer woke Major Anderson and reported that a strange ship was entering the harbor. Anderson scrambled from his bed and pulled on his uniform. The appearance of the ship surprised everyone in the fort because they did not know that the president had sent supplies. Anderson quickly ordered his men to their guns.

The *Star of the West* continued toward the fort. An officer from a secessionist battery examined the ship through a telescope. He realized that it was carrying supplies to Fort Sumter.

Everyone in the harbor tensely watched the ship. It seemed inevitable that someone would fire the first shot—which would almost certainly result in a full-scale war.

The officer from the secessionist battery could not allow the United States government to reinforce the soldiers at Fort Sumter. "Fire!" he shouted. The secession artillery fired several quick shots. The red-hot shells streaked over the harbor and crashed into the

water around the *Star of the West*. The captain of the ship frantically looked toward Fort Sumter. If the fort did not return fire, then the ship could be destroyed.

The secessionists fired upon the Star of the West *in an attempt to keep the ship from reaching Fort Sumter.*

At Fort Sumter, the soldiers waited for Major Anderson's order to return the fire. But Anderson did not give the order because he didn't want to be responsible for starting the war.

The secessionist shelling of the *Star of the West* continued, becoming more accurate. Suddenly a shell came skipping over the water. It slammed into the *Star of the West* and exploded. The captain, realizing that the soldiers at Fort Sumter would not return the fire, ordered the ship to retreat from the harbor.

The people of Charleston cheered the victory. But South Carolina's leaders soon realized that they had acted too quickly. No other Southern state had yet seceded from the Union. South Carolina could not fight a war against the United States alone. Governor Pickens and other leaders backed down from their earlier demands for a surrender of Fort Sumter. Charleston enjoyed a brief—but uneasy—peace.

Soon other Southern leaders who wanted to follow South Carolina's lead gathered to debate secession. Mississippi, Louisiana, Florida, Alabama, and Georgia all seceded from the Union by the end of January 1861. The Southern states quickly formed their own country called the Confederate States of America. On February 18, Jefferson Davis became president of the Confederacy. As the new president, Davis took control of the Fort Sumter crisis. He ordered an

Jefferson Davis

Jefferson Davis was inaugurated as the president of the Confederate States of America on February 18, 1861.

officer, General Pierre Beauregard, to surround Fort Sumter with fortifications and batteries. Beauregard promised to put Fort Sumter in "a ring of fire."

The Confederate States of America quickly seized all United States property and forts within its borders. During February and March, President Buchanan watched helplessly as federal property and U.S. authority were taken under control by the Confederacy. Only Fort Sumter and another fort in Florida remained in Union hands. The country was gripped by the crisis, and people everywhere anxiously waited for Abraham Lincoln to take office.

President-elect Abraham Lincoln arrived in Washington, D.C., at the end of February. On March 4, 1861, Lincoln took the presidential oath of office. While reading his inaugural address to the nation, Lincoln promised "to hold, occupy and possess all property and places belonging to the government." This meant that President Lincoln would not allow the Confederacy to seize Fort Sumter without a fight.

The next morning, Lincoln arrived in the White House to find a letter on his desk from Major Anderson. It stated that Fort Sumter had

enough food for only six more weeks. Unless
the fort received more supplies, Anderson
would be forced to surrender the fort to the
Confederacy.

Lincoln called his cabinet together to debate
the situation at Fort Sumter. The members of
the president's cabinet are his closest advisers,
and he always asks for their opinions before he
makes any big decisions.

One of Lincoln's advisers passionately
proclaimed, "The Union must be preserved. If
we evacuate the fort, then the Union is dead."

Another adviser disagreed. "An expedition to
supply Sumter would cause a war." He argued
that the Union struggle to retain control of
Fort Sumter was a lost cause. The debate
lasted for weeks.

Lincoln and the members of his cabinet debated the situation at Fort Sumter for several weeks before Lincoln decided to send another supply ship.

Lincoln was also deeply concerned about the rest of the South. Virginia, North Carolina, Tennessee, Maryland, and other Southern states had not yet seceded from the Union. Lincoln worried that if he tried to reinforce Fort Sumter, then these states might decide to join the Confederacy. But if Lincoln allowed the fort to be captured, he knew that he would suffer from enormous criticism by the citizens of the Northern states.

Finally, on April 4, Lincoln reached a decision. He ordered a supply ship to reinforce Fort Sumter. He knew that the action could lead to war, but he had promised to protect government property, and he meant to keep his vow.

This map of the United States in April 1861, shows the six Southern states that had already seceeded from the Union, and the states that Lincoln feared would join the Confederacy.

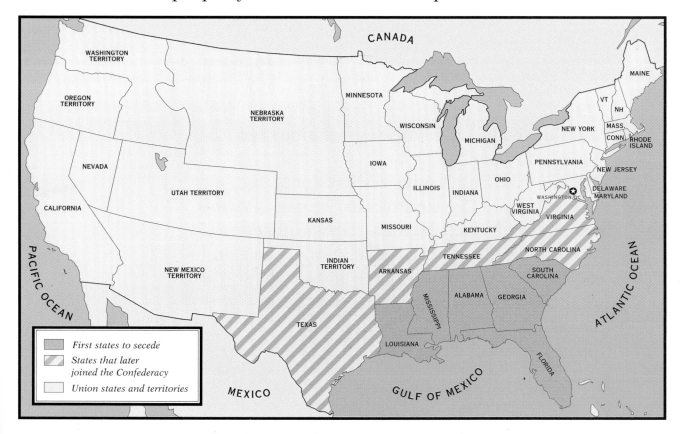

Meanwhile, in Fort Sumter, Major Anderson became increasingly discouraged. The fort's food supply was dwindling, and his small unit could not work all of the guns at the same time. More than one hundred Confederate guns were constantly pointed at Fort Sumter from Charleston. At night, thousands of campfires along the shore reminded the soldiers in the fort that they were cut off from the outside world.

Confederate president Jefferson Davis soon received the news that Lincoln had sent a supply ship to the fort. The Confederates could wait no longer. Davis ordered Pierre Beauregard to capture Fort Sumter.

General Pierre Beauregard

On April 11, Beauregard sent three messengers with a letter to Major Anderson demanding that the fort be surrendered immediately. In a note to Beauregard, Anderson replied that he would not give up his post.

But Anderson did not feel as confident as his note implied. The emotional strain of the last four months had left him exhausted. Anderson gave his reply to the three Confederate messengers, and walked with them back to their boat. On the way, Anderson asked, "Will Beauregard give us a warning before he opens fire?" The messengers assured Anderson that Beauregard would issue a warning. Anderson heard the answer and blurted, "If you do not batter us to pieces, we will be starved out in a few days."

The Confederates were surprised by the major's response. Certain that Anderson would be forced to surrender when he ran out of food, Beauregard told Jefferson Davis about the meeting with Anderson. But Davis was unconvinced. He ordered Beauregard to attack Fort Sumter.

At 3:20 A.M. on April 12, Beauregard sent the warning message to Major Anderson. "We have the honor to notify you that we will open the fire of our batteries on Fort Sumter in one hour from this time." Anderson and his officers woke the soldiers, and ordered them into the fort's bombproof shelter.

At 4:30 A.M., a cannon was fired from the Confederate batteries. The shell arched gracefully into the air before it slowly descended and exploded over the fort. The shot was a signal to the other Confederate guns to open fire.

In a mighty roar, every Confederate gun in the harbor fired at the fort. The dark night lit up with the bright streaks of shells and bombs. Crowds gathered on the roofs and church steeples of Charleston to watch the bombardment. The fort disappeared behind a cloud of smoke, explosions, and harbor spray kicked up by the shells. But the Confederate gun crews were very inexperienced. Many of the shells exploded harmlessly above the fort or fell hissing into the harbor. The fort's thick walls protected the soldiers inside.

In order to get a better view, many of the citizens of Charleston watched the bombardment of Fort Sumter from their rooftops.

As the sun rose, Anderson ordered his men to eat breakfast and prepare for battle. But Anderson faced serious problems. He had more guns than he could fire, and the fort had very little ammunition. He ordered the men to return their fire slowly, in order to conserve ammunition.

As the day wore on, the Confederate shells began to cause damage to the fort. Confederate soldiers heated the shells until they were red-hot. When these shells landed on buildings inside the fort, they began to burn. Choking smoke filled the fort as the Union soldiers fought to extinguish the fires. The brick walls of the fort began to crumble under the repeated pounding from the shells. Throughout the day, the U.S. soldiers and the Confederates exchanged fire. By the evening, Major Anderson and his men were exhausted. Anderson's only hope was that relief would arrive soon from the North.

The Civil War officially began on the morning of April 12, 1861, with the Confederate attack on Fort Sumter.

But Lincoln's relief expedition could not break through the bombardment. Helplessly, the ships watched as Fort Sumter endured the shelling.

By the next morning (April 13), thick black smoke poured from the fort as the Confederates increased their artillery fire. Anderson began to see that the fort's situation was hopeless. Clearly, Union supplies would not be able to get through. It was only a matter of time before the Confederate guns reduced the fort to rubble. Early in the afternoon, exhausted and low on food, Anderson ordered his men to display the white flag of surrender. Beauregard ordered the Confederates to stop firing, and an eerie silence settled over the harbor.

Red-hot shells launched by the Confederate artillery sparked fires throughout the fort.

Confederate leaders quickly rowed out to Fort Sumter. As they entered the smoldering fort, they offered Anderson their conditions of surrender. Anderson accepted, relieved that no one had been killed in the bombardment. The Confederates allowed Anderson to lower the American flag with full military honors. But during the ceremony a shell accidentally exploded, killing a Union soldier. It was the first death of what came to be known as the first battle of the Civil War.

Following Anderson's surrender, the Confederates marked their victory by raising South Carolina's flag inside Fort Sumter.

With a Confederate band playing "Yankee Doodle Dandy," Anderson and his men boarded a ship that would return them to New York. As the flag of South Carolina rose above Fort

Sumter, the Confederate batteries fired a jubilant salute.

News of the surrender of Fort Sumter to the Confederacy spread rapidly throughout the nation. A Southerner wrote that Fort Sumter's surrender "sent a thrill of joy to the heart of every true friend of the South. The face of every Southerner was brighter than it had been before."

Lincoln heard the news on the afternoon of April 14. He considered the bombardment to be an act of war. The next day he issued a call for volunteers to crush the Confederate rebellion. Throughout the North, thousands volunteered to fight in the Union army.

Anticipating full-scale civil war, President Lincoln issued a call for volunteers to join the Union army.

By the end of the war (1865), all that remained of Fort Sumter were crumbling walls, charred wood, and piles of bricks.

In the South, however, people reacted angrily to Lincoln's call for Union volunteers. Virginia, North Carolina, Tennessee, and Arkansas refused to send troops. They soon joined the Confederacy, and thousands of Southerners excitedly prepared for war.

Two years later, in 1863, a combination of Union navy and army units attempted to retake Fort Sumter. The Union fleet bombarded the fort for months. Much of the fort was reduced to rubble, but the Confederate garrison fought bravely. The Union attacks failed, and Fort Sumter remained under Confederate control.

During the first weeks of April 1865, four long and destructive years after the first battle at Fort

Sumter, the Civil War ended. The North was victorious. On April 14, Robert Anderson returned to Fort Sumter to take part in a ceremony that would mark the return of the fort to Union control. It had been exactly four years since he had surrendered Fort Sumter to the Confederates. Anderson hardly recognized it. Heaps of rubble and piles of charred wood and bricks were all that remained.

Anderson mounted a platform in the middle of what was left of the fort.

On April 14, 1865, Major Anderson returned to the fort and raised the same American flag over Fort Sumter that he had been forced to take down in surrender four years earlier.

Under his arm, he carried the same United States flag that he had taken down in surrender four years earlier. In a voice shaking with emotion, Anderson addressed the crowd: "I thank God that I have lived to see this day." He carefully attached the flag to the flagpole, and slowly raised it over the fort. As the flag waved in the breeze, one hundred guns fired a salute to celebrate the end of the war.

GLOSSARY

battery

bombardment

battery – collection of guns, cannons, and other artillery assembled for battle

bombardment – an attack with heavy gunfire

cabinet – group of advisers for the head of a government

economy – the way a state runs its goods and services

fleet – group of ships

fortification – building erected to strengthen a military position

garrison – central location where many soldiers are located

immigrant – person who comes from one country to live permanently in another country

plantation – large farm that usually specializes in growing one crop

president-elect – the person who has won a presidential election but has not yet been sworn in to office

rebellion – armed fight against a government

shell – small bomb that is fired from a cannon

strategy – plan for winning a battle or achieving a goal

tactics – the methods used to win a battle

traitor – person who betrays his or her country

TIMELINE

1860

November: Abraham Lincoln elected president

December: South Carolina secedes from Union, Anderson moves his men to Fort Sumter

1861

January: Star of the West driven away from Fort Sumter

February: Jefferson Davis becomes president of Confederacy

March: Lincoln pledges to protect federal property

April 4: Lincoln orders supply ships to Fort Sumter

April 11: Beauregard demands Anderson's surrender

April 12: Confederates fire on Fort Sumter

April 13: Anderson surrenders Fort Sumter

April 15: Lincoln calls for volunteers

1863 Union attempts to retake Fort Sumter

1865 *April:* Confederate army surrenders, ending Civil War

INDEX *(**Boldface** page numbers indicate illustrations.)*

PHOTO CREDITS

©: Archive Photos: 8 bottom, 18, 19, 29, 31 bottom right; Corbis-Bettmann: 3, 5 right, 8 top, 10, 11, 12, 13, 15, 17, 21, 24, 27, 28, 31 left; Massachusetts Commandery Military Order of the Loyal Legion and the US Army Military History Institute: 1; National Archives: 6; North Wind Picture Archives: 7, 9, 23, 25, 30; Stock Montage, Inc.: 4 (Historical Pictures); Superstock, Inc.: 2; UPI/Corbis-Bettmann: 5 left, 16, 22, 26, 31 top right.

Maps by TJS Design.

ABOUT THE AUTHOR

Brendan January was born and raised in Pleasantville, New York. He attended Haverford College in Pennsylvania, where he earned his B.A. in History and English. An Abraham Lincoln enthusiast, he has written three books for the Cornerstones of Freedom series, *The Emancipation Proclamation, Fort Sumter,* and *The Lincoln-Douglas Debates.* Mr. January divides his time between New York City and Danbury, Connecticut.